Things I Learned in the Night

Emily Byrnes

DEDICATION

To all of my students, past and present. You are strong and smart and full of potential. You matter, always, even when you feel like you don't.

New Lebanon Jr/Sr High

Utica Academy of Science

Little Falls Middle School

Contents

Contents

I have a whole world
tucked away in my closet;
sepia colored memories
of my parents in the eighties,
ticket stubs from movies I don't remember
because I was too busy exploring the mouth
of a boy I do,
and crinkled petals from a golden sunflower
that said you still love me.

And though you haven't come back yet,
I know you will,
because sunflowers
never lie.

Sunflowers Never Lie

We watched the horizon
as the evening sun spun the clouds
into sugar pink and baby blue.
It was then
that your thigh grazed mine
for the first time,
just one day in mid-July
but it felt infinite
like we were as never ending
as the cotton candy sky.

Cotton Candy Sky

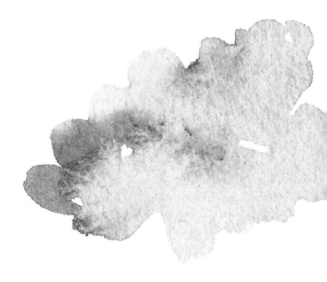

I watched her drop a mug,
pick up each piece
and glue it back together
like it was the holy grail.

I fell in love that day,
not because she was clumsy or cute,
but because she still saw value
in something so broken.

The time I fell in love in a coffee shop

We dig for answers
for meaning
for truth
like little voles
scrabbling underground to safety
not knowing the foxes
have already dug out
the other end of the tunnel.

By the time we find the answer,
it's usually too late.

Digging

Now I know
how terrified the caterpillar feels
when he crafts his cocoon;
his little body changing,
no one telling him how
or why
or when it will stop.

I wonder,
will I metamorphosize,
or die inside this chrysalis they call adolescence
with sticky wet wings that will never get the chance
to unfurl and feel the sun.

Caterpillars and Butterflies

Your fingertips
touch mine,
just a brush, but
magic
and I imagine
what it would be like
if they touched my cheek
or my neck
or the skin between my crop top
and jeans.

Delicious.

Discovering Feels

It's the three little dots that keep popping up on the corner of my screen just after I say *I think I love you.* I'm pushing up daisies, dead in the ground, and you're just taking your sweet time.

A 2018 Anxiety Attack

I sleep at night
and dream
and my dreams embarrass me
because I long
for something I've never known-
ocean blue eyes, a fleeting touch, a slow kiss
I wake up covered in hot sweat
and everything aches so wonderfully
like muscles during a good stretch.

What is this feeling?
I'm not sure it's human.

Awakening

See the tree roots,
how they've been scabbed and scarred
by clumsy feet
and lawn mowers that rode too close?
See how we pound and batter them
but still they grow and fuel the air
so that we may breathe
and shelter us from the hot, red sun.

Their love is unconditional
and we are children of the Earth
who've not yet learned
to appreciate our mother.

Earth Day Thoughts

We held hands
with our fingers laced like corsets
that fit so perfectly
so snugly
I could hardly breathe.

First Date

Dig
scratch
tear away the earth
with broken nails and scarred knuckles.
Let dirt cake your fingers
like grout between two tiles
wipe the sweat off your forehead
with dirty paws
and let mud stain your sweaty brow.

Push the little seed down,
wait for the rain,
and I promise with all my heart
that something beautiful will grow.

Planting

He buys Aztec shirts
from thrift stores
(though his father pays his rent)
and wears round-rimmed glasses
like it's 1969.
He thinks Socialism
and minimalism
are the answer to everything
and reads Kurt Vonnegut in public
but comic books at home
while he pretends to enjoy the taste of whiskey.
He's thin and handsome and educated
but the only thing he ever taught me
was how to

R U N.

The Modern Day Playboy

The moon rises over the city
and they crawl out of dens half-naked
howling with desire
craving the flesh of women
they hardly know.
Dying not to be alone,
they won't even regret the innocent hearts
they feast on in the night.

It's hard to tell men
from werewolves these days.

Werewolves in the City

You kiss like caramel.

Sticky sweet,
it melts in my mouth
and always leaves me wanting more.

Give Me Sugar

Down the path,
through the gate
into the garden of Eden.
I'm no Eve,
but I know which fruits
are forbidden at fifteen.
But look how juicy, look how sweet;
maybe a bite *is* worth
eternal suffering,
after all.

Desire

Grasshopper in the garden,
you hop from leaf to leaf
stringing me along with my little net.
You like this game, don't you?
Because you know I cannot win.

But I learned a trick, see.
If I walk by without a net
uninterestedly,
I can trap you with bare hands.

What the grasshopper taught me about men

They tell us spontaneous combustion
is a myth,
but they cannot explain
how he lit me on fire
from the inside out.

Burn

I want to lay in the freshly mowed grass and be young again. I want to take off my shoes and stain my clothes green and eat dinner without washing my hands. I want to go to bed with pollen in my hair and the windows open and the sound of rain. I want to wake up eight or ten or twelve again. But when I wake it's not right. This isn't my mother's house, and nobody is here to clean up my messes. I miss you, I miss you. I miss the way the sky looked before I grew tall and the sound of my voice before it grew tired. Take me back, just take me back.

I can still hear
moon shadow, moon shadow
in my mother's voice,
like twenty-five years ago
was just yesterday
and I am still a little girl
fighting off sleep,
begging for one more song.

Lullaby

I've always liked the way *darling* sounded;
like coming home to snug, warm arms
after a long day's work.

Like a newborn baby
crying in a lace-trimmed crib
in a little room with pale yellow walls.

Like security.
Like enough to get by.
Like a home I'd never want to flee.

It was so easy to get lost in you,
Darling.
like walking through the woods without a compass,
and finding the River Styx,
touching eternal water
(your skin, lips, below your waist)
and never, ever going back.

My Love, My Dreams, My Everything

We grow round and supple with age;
a little thicker in the thighs,
a bit rounder in the middle.
We are so full,
yet we look in the mirror and
try to convince ourselves
we're not pretty anymore
because the magazines tell us
our soft and our stretch marks
aren't beautiful.

But go to the mango tree,
seek out a fruit,
and tell me you won't pick the
fullest, ripest one.

Ripe

My hands became a home
to a tiny bird once
who'd been thrown from the nest
in the dead of night.

That little bird was left unwanted
so I took her in and showed her love
and fed her sugar water
and encouraged her to sing.

Now, she fills my yard with sweet songs
that quell my sadness
and I finally understand
that karma isn't magic,
it's the action of reaping what you sow.

Songbird

Legs
spread like bird wings
hoping to fly away
with him
or her
or whomever will listen
because the world never did
and now
this is the only way
she knows how to talk.

Legs

I learned how to sneak out windows
and into your brother's car without waking
the neighbor's dog.

How to kiss with my tongue
and lie with crossed fingers
when my friends ask where I am.
He's no good for you
they'd say again and again,
but I learned how to hear without listening.

How to feel an entire ocean of waves
rocking through my body like a beautiful storm with
just a touch of your hands in the right place.

How to undress in the dark
and lose myself in sweet summer nights
scent of lilacs, chirping of spring peepers in the pond
and believe you when you say *I love you,*
I love you more than I've ever loved anything.

How to hide the tears in my eyes when I learn
that's just something boys say *in the moment*
and how to pretend to be okay with that
when I've given you all I have to give.

How to ride in a passenger seat in deafening silence
when all I can think about is screaming,
and how to close the door quietly when
I want so badly to slam it into the earth.

How to tiptoe up the stairs without waking the house,
who will tattle-tale with creaks and moans if I step in the
wrong place.

How to crawl into my bed like an injured dog
and lick my wounds;
my pride, my innocence, my heart.

And finally, how to tell when boys like you
use sweet little lies like skeleton keys
to get inside of girls like me
when all we want is to be loved
and feel special and not so very alone.

Things I Learned in the Night

I left you out in the rain
and just as I feared,
you complained about
wet socks
and matted hair
and ruined shoes
but never once exclaimed
how great it was to be alive.

You're Not Like Me

--TW: mentions suicide--

I ugly cry over him in the hallway and the teacher tells me not to weep over someone who will not matter in a year or two or ten. The bell rings and I sit down, red in the face, trying to forget. She says *Open up Shakespeare; page 168,* and I read about a thirteen year old who kills herself over a boy she knew for twenty-four hours. The teacher says *"isn't it poetic"* and *"can't you* feel *their pain"* and I want to scream *how the hell is that love!?* because I loved a boy for five months and twenty-seven days and I didn't kill myself but it nearly killed me. But I don't ask because I already know the answer; young love only means something when it's written by adults.

Juliet

I grow wildflowers from my back
like a fertile garden
and you pick them one by one
until I am all bare roots
and broken stems.
You pluck the petals-
She loves me, she loves me not
but that's the problem, see;
I'm kneeling at your feet,
offering you the skin off my back
and still you need an old wives' tale
to prove that it's enough.

Plucking Petals

She came to me in a dream,
fluid as water,
solid as a stone.
I reach for her
and wonder
what the color pink tastes like
and whether her skin is softer than the rain
but I don't get to find out
because you cannot feel a rainstorm
when you're already wet.

Curious

I once read something that went like this:

"If you are looking for a sign to stay, here is your sign."

So I am just reiterating these words
in case you haven't heard them before:

Stay

Stay

Stay

STAY.

(There's a reason you're here. There is meaning in your
journey. There is recovery. There are better brain days.
There are fewer tears. There are smiles that aren't so forced.
There is happiness. Believe that.)

Make every footfall blend in with the air
like a doe who walks through an open field at night.
Hold your breath,
climb the ladder
-carefully, quietly-
up to my open window;
an invitation only for you.

Speak slow and soft,
-pretend it hurts to talk-
and kiss my mouth
like we're saying goodbye for the last time
even though we both know
you'll be back again tomorrow.

While Our Parents Slept

We stayed out past curfew and shut our phones off
(we were all we needed then)
and you showed me Nada Surf
and Canis Major and how to feel safe in someone else's arms.
We didn't need a skylight,
just the roof of the Honda Odyssey your parents
let you drive on the weekend.
Hand in hand,
we talked about our hopes and dreams and fears
as if they were Andromeda;
light years away.

We didn't know what *imminent* meant,
how quickly three months could pass,
or how distance can tear two people apart
even if they are soulmates.
(We didn't know that the universe
can change *are* to *were,* either.)
I couldn't see anything past
the tip of your nose as it grazed mine or
the little puffs of fog our breath made
as we talked that cold, violet night.

No, I couldn't see anything but you.

Andromeda

Please don't blame me for running;
the universe has lit so many fires under my feet
I've been conditioned to flee
at the sign of a spark.

Pavlov's Dog

Your soul erupted from blank space
with the supernovas and the stars.
It has lived a hundred thousand lives
as all different creatures
over a million different years;
do not presume
it has only one mate.

There will be Another

It could be worse
doesn't make it feel any better now,
does it?

Unhelpful Help

His arms surround me
like a nice, yellow house.
A warm house,
a safe house,
probably in the suburbs
with a white picket fence.
But your arms;
they were a home.
A home with an old soul
(maybe a lake house in the fall)
with a wood stove and kitchenette
and a murphy bed imprinted with bodies
shaped like ours.
Granted, there were a few leaks here and there,
and the wind got in at night,
but I don't remember ever feeling cold.

My head wants the house,
but no matter how I try,
my heart just wants to go home.

The heart wants what it wants

The strong arms of September
slam into the door of the sun room
and threaten to tear us apart,
like warm dinner rolls fresh from the oven;
breaking bread for warm soup and cold, lonely nights;
winter specialties.

I do not want to give you up
just because summer
is coming to an end.

Summer Fling

He tells me he will hibernate
like the wood toads and the bees
and will not wake up
until we're together again.

I go back to school
and wonder if he dreams of me
the way I dream of him.

Summer Boy

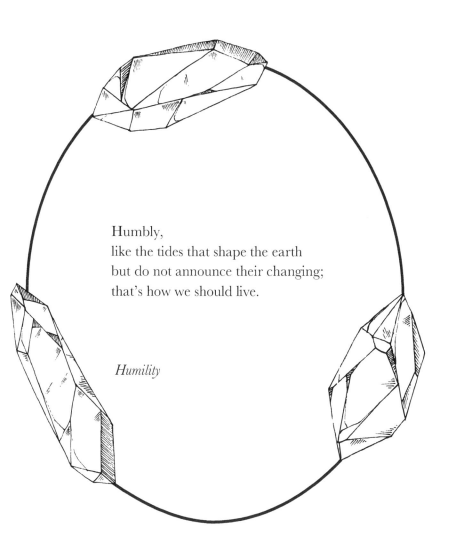

Humbly,
like the tides that shape the earth
but do not announce their changing;
that's how we should live.

Humility

If the river drowned you,
would you say it was out of love?
Was Vesuvius romantic
just because two lovers died in each other's arms,
preserved in ash for all time?

The answer to those questions is no,
so why do we keep using love to justify pain?

Love Does Not Hurt

They say
it doesn't matter whether it was real to them
if it was real to **you**

as if I'm a child
with an imaginary friend
and I'm supposed to feel good
about creating a narrative
no one else wanted a part in
at twenty-three years old.

More Unhelpful Help

*She's just a frien*d
you said
so I invited her in and offered her
my coffee, my friendship, and my couch
but then she took you
right out from under me
and now she lives in the house
I used to call home
and sleeps with the man
I used to call my own
like a cuckoo
who lays its eggs
in another bird's nest
and watches
as it single-handedly destroys a family
and justifies it with instinct.

Cuckoo Bird

It was like watching a flickering candle
near an open window;
we knew our flame was going to burn out,
we just didn't know how long it would take.

One year, two months, and seventeen days

She talked to me
as though we had never touched,
as if getting too colloquial
might lead to intimacy.
But just being in her presence was intimate for me,
I felt naked, fully clothed
and speechless
though words poured out of me
like sloppy rain from overflowing gutters.

It's funny how similar the end can feel
to the beginning,
the only difference is that now
my stomach is in knots because I'm dying a little
with each second that ticks by
and then, I was just being born
like Aphrodite from the shell;
innocent into a world full of want.

Tension

He used to hold my face in his hands
and say *you'll always be my Konstantine*
but he just knew the words,
he didn't know the meaning.
He didn't know one day
I'd cut off my blonde hair
and paint it black
or cry in the mornings
for no reason at all.

We grew up
we grew apart
because forever is so easy
at eighteen
and so easy to forget
by twenty three.

Konstantine, who?
You don't even remember,
do you?
Just some pretty words that
slipped out after sex.

Konstantine

Camels and wildebeest and mountain goats,
the predators that hunt them,
and you.

Nomads

I outgrew you,
shed you like an exoskeleton,
left you stuck to the concrete in the dead of summer,
shiny skin blistering in the heat.

I guess you could say I'm more cicada than butterfly.

Cicada

Open the window and let the rain in. Let it soak the books on the windowsill (we never read them, anyway) and let us drown in white noise before the flood comes to carry us away.

I guess this is what the end feels like; like pretending we're enjoying the rain, when really we're just hoping it fills the silence so we don't have to.

The End

I look at him
and he looks right through me,
as if he is trying to unsee me.

As if I never even mattered
just because I do not matter now.

As if girls just give away love like
a pile of worn clothes to charity,
expecting nothing in return.

The First Break

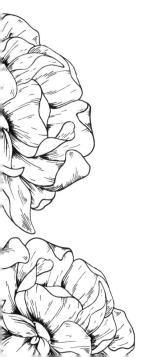

Rain pounds on the windows
but I feel it in my bones
like steel bullets
knock-knock-knocking on my spine.
It's almost fitting,
like a movie,
except there is no plane
and you wouldn't stop me from getting on it,
anyway.

Not a Movie

It's funny how boring normalcy seems
until it is ripped away.

Things we take for granted

You and I were sinew
connected like muscle to bone.

But as with all organic things,
the fibers aged and weakened
and somehow
staying together after high school
started to feel a lot like
being caught in the sticky web of a spider
who wasn't even hungry for my flesh
anymore.

Connective Tissue

You stuck a feeding tube
down my throat and into my gut
the day you said
I think we're better off as friends.
It's uncomfortable and foreign and just *there.*
I'm surviving,
but there's no enjoyment
and I have to wonder
why the universe
would dangle something so perfect in front of me
if I cannot indulge in it a little.

Just Friends

He comes back after three long years
and wants to try again.

I say it would be like
planting flowers we knew we couldn't sow,
but he says
why transplant the bulbs when we already know the soil is fertile
and the climate is good and arable?
and I have to think that maybe he's right.

That maybe three years apart
has made our thumbs a little greener.

Touché

Mederma for my scars,
foundation on my chin,
dark jeans on a hot summer day
because I don't like the color of my legs.

Do you do it, too?
Do you cloak your insecurities
and hope they don't show through?

Cloaked

For world peace, of course,
for an island full of dogs,
and for your voice to crack and burn like hot fire in your
throat every time you speak my name.

I want you to know how it feels to have my name
seared on your tongue
but not be able to do anything about it.

If I had Three Wishes...

Like a worn blanket,
a bad hand of cards,
or flour into egg.

I fold into you easily
as if we belong
under
on top of
all over one another.

Fold

I've always loved order;
schedules, plans, ducks in a row.

But you are scattered all over
like rainbow pieces of a kaleidoscope
and I'm starting to think
there's something to be said
for chaos.

Type A

Listen to the songs that hurt;
they belong to you.

He may have gotten the dog
and the apartment
and your friends,
but he's not getting
Bon Iver.

Bom Iver

I flip through the yellowing pages
of a paperback book by Steinbeck
that cost someone 99¢ in 1981
and it dawns on me;
I'm just like poor Lennie.

I love too hard
and watch it die
and never, ever understand why.

Of Mice and Men

I bought these shoes for work
and all of a sudden it's three years later
and I'm still wearing them,
still complaining that they give me ingrown toenails
but never doing anything about it.

I'm like that, sometimes.
I measure time by clothes that've gone out of style
and speeding tickets the insurance company
has finally let go
and food that's expired in the back of the fridge
(has it been a week already?)

Clocks and calendars are for fools
who think they have any control,
so I just let time slip by
and pretend everything was "just yesterday"
so I don't feel like I'm speeding
toward the finish line,
because who the hell knows
where the finish line is,
anyway.

Clocks and Calendars

Look at the storm, you said. See how the sky turns Poseidon blue and the waves crest white like Tibetan mountains? You said *come, let's go outside and feel it* but I was too busy boarding up windows and checking flashlights to notice. You held out your hand and said I'd never see the beauty in life wearing glasses made of fear, but I didn't take it. I've been hurt enough to know that when the storm alarm sounds, I've got to put up my walls or get out.

How I Live Through Hurricanes

There's an old saying
about a horse and some water
and a man who leads him to it.

I used to think the horse was dumb
(we're meant to, aren't we?)
but men are always giving me things
and then expecting me
to sip and swallow at their feet.

Maybe
the horse just wanted someone to walk with.

Maybe
he wasn't even thirsty.

Interpretations

Alcohol in my cut
It hurts I scream and jump
like fire ants have crawled inside me.

My mother says to count to ten
so I do but the pain is still there.
Count to ten again
and by the time I reach seven or eight
I start to forget
like she knew I would.

Maybe it will be ten breaths
or ten months
or ten years
but eventually,
if I just keep counting,
the pain from you will fade away
and you will be a tiny scar
or a little mark
or if I'm lucky,

nothing
at
all.

Count to Ten

I find you in all the parts of me I'm too afraid to let go of. Like the long hair I cannot bring myself to cut and the dirty hands I refuse to wash because they are the last parts of me you touched. I find you in those places and forget that part of growing is always l e t t i n g   g o.

Let Go

"Johnny"

An allegory. A memoir. Maybe.

His name was Johnny
and I met him near the tree
whose branches wept long, sad tears just like me.

I was just a girl then, lying in the grass
soaking up sunlight, letting time pass
and that's when I heard him
over bullfrogs and bees
I heard his voice,
calling only to me.

Come to the forest,
come,
come....

Never trust strangers
my mother's voice said
they just lead to danger
but I ignored her and went
as fast as I could (I was bored, see)
on dirty hands and scabby knees
through the Tanglewood, into the trees.

He waited for me
like he promised he would,
he sat like a frog
near a hut made of wood.

He had blue skin
and yellow eyes of a cat,
watching, looking for love;
his eyes were like that.

Why are you sad?
I asked him with heart
remembering how hard it is
to feel torn apart.

No mother, no father, no sisters, he said
just trees and a world feeling terribly dead.
So I patted his back saying *you're not alone*
though you might feel it
being all on your own.

Here's not the problem
he said, *it's out **there**.*
Haven't you noticed that very few care?

I went home that night
having made a new friend,
sat down for a bite
as day came to an end.

I talked and talked about my day in the wood
and mom said *mmhmm* and dad said *that's good.*
But they didn't listen,
just scrolled through their phones
and I started to wonder
was *I* on my own?

I went back to Johnny the very next day
(back into the trees; I remembered the way)
and said *I think I'm alone, I'm alone just like you*
and his eyes opened wide and his skin sparkled blue.

He patted my back and said
at least you have me; now I have you too.

We played in the forest from day into night
and he showed me the creatures,
the ones who didn't bite.
We made daisy chains and found fairy rings,
we jumped and we swam and did all sorts of things.

This is how it was for us, before tech came along
before, when we knew better where we belonged
I belong to the forest,
I belong to the trees;
I'm at home in the mud,
in the grass, with the bees.

And that was the summer I first fell in love
with Johnny, with life, with the sky up above.
I went home each night to *mmhmms* and *that's goods*
and counted the hours till the next day in the woods.

But summer came and summer went in a blur,
and before I knew it, along came September
Back to school mother said
with your books and your friends;
how quickly that summer had come to the end.

I'll miss you, Johnny
I said *see you soon*
before we know it, it'll be June.
I'll come back again and here we can play

as long as you promise, oh promise to stay.

But he slipped away at summer's end
and I grew up, forgot, never saw him again.
I grew into parties and Snapchat and boys;
I forgot about nature and simpler joys.

Like all kids today,
I grew up too quickly,
I ran from my youth
and moved to the city.
As a grown up I did all I possibly could,
but I never had fun like I did in those woods.

So stay young while you can,
keep your imagination
keep your wonder, your joy,
your drive for creation.

Was Johnny real?
I'll never say
but he taught me one thing
I keep with me each day;
enjoy the wind and the trees and get out in the sun,
because 'ere you know it,
this life will be done.

And years later,
Alice returned to Wonderland
to find that nothing was quite the same.

*Because growing up and moving on
can do that to a person.*

Alice

Things I Learned in the Night

ABOUT THE AUTHOR

Emily Byrnes is from Dolgeville, NY where she spent her childhood surrounded by a loving family, fresh country air, and the woods. She holds a BA in Literature from Siena College and an MA in Education from Utica College. She currently resides in Troy, NY with her husband and their rescue dog, Pepper. As well as being a writer, Emily teaches English Language Arts in New Lebanon, NY to some of the coolest middle schoolers on the planet. She is an advocate for mental health and wellness, especially in kids and teens, a dog lover, and a vegan. She can be found on Instagram @by.emilybyrnes and loves to connect with her wonderful readers.

Also by Emily Byrnes:

Poetry:

A Strangely Wrapped Gift

Swim

Journals:

One Day at a Time (a guided bullet journal)

One Breath at a Time (a guided bullet journal for anxiety)

The Self-Care Project (for teens)

Everything by Emily Byrnes can be found on Amazon.com worldwide and many other online /in store retailers. Please leave a review if you find something you love <3

FOLLOW ON INSTAGRAM: @BY.EMILYBYRNES

(FACEBOOK AND TWITTER, TOO!)

28993831R00052

Made in the USA
Columbia, SC
19 October 2018